GET INFORMED, STAY INFORMED

NET NEUTRALITY

Natalie Hyde

CRABTREE
PUBLISHING COMPANY
WWW.CRABTREEBOOKS.COM

Author: Natalie Hyde
Series Research and Development:
Reagan Miller
Editor-in-Chief: Lionel Bender
Editor: Ellen Rodger
Proofreaders: Laura Booth,
Wendy Scavuzzo
Project coordinator: Petrice Custance
Design and photo research:
Ben White
Production: Kim Richardson
Print coordinator: Katherine Berti
Consultant: Emily Drew,
The New York Public Library

Produced for Crabtree
Publishing Company by
Bender Richardson White

Photographs and reproductions:
Alamy
Michael Candelori: p. 4 (bottom)
NetPhotos: p. 16–17
Newscom: p. 12–13, 36–37
Newsies Media: p. 37
Sergio Azenha: p. 42–43
sjscreens: p. 30–31
Getty Images
Alexander Nemenov/AFP:
p. 28–29
Brooks Kraft: p. 34–35
Chip Somodevilla: p. 6–7
Drew Angerer: p. 40–41
George Frey/Bloomberg: p. 24–25
Philippe Huguen/AFP: p. 18–19
Scott Eisen/Bloomberg: p. 32–33
Smith Collection/Gado: p. 20–21
Shutterstock: box icons, cover,
heading band, p. 10–11, 22–23
bluebay: p. 1
Byrkl_foto: p. 4 (top)
Casezy idea: p. 21
Dmytro Zinkevych: p. 26–27
Dusan Petkovic: p. 19

Lukassek: p. 24
Mark Van Scyoc: p. 8–9
Nata–Lia: p. 17
NicoElNino: p. 14–15
rawpixel.com: p. 23
skyNext: p. 35
Teguh Jati Prasetyo: p. 7
withGod: p. 38–39
Diagrams: Stefan Chabluk, using
the following as sources of data:
p. 7 National Cable Television
Association/www.boingboing.net; p. 12
Federal Communications Commission;
p. 14 www.steemit.com/cybermedios.
org; p.16 The Washington Post/Netflix;
p. 22 www.PureVPN.com/blog; p.25
Akamai State of the Internet/www.ncta.
com; p. 26 Open Technology Institute,
New America Foundation; p. 29 LA
Times business section; p. 32 www.
theatlas.com/search/ISPs Bureau of
Labor Statistics. p. https://tinyurl.
com/ya4nu7yc; p. 39 www.speedtest.
net/global-index; p. 43 Max Woolf/
minimaxir.com

Library and Archives Canada Cataloguing in Publication

Hyde, Natalie, 1963-, author
Net neutrality / Natalie Hyde.

(Get informed--stay informed)
Includes bibliographical references and index.
Issued in print and electronic formats.
ISBN 978-0-7787-4968-4 (hardcover).--
ISBN 978-0-7787-4972-1 (softcover).--
ISBN 978-1-4271-2121-9 (HTML)

1. Network neutrality--Juvenile literature. 2. Internet
governance--Juvenile literature. 3. Telecommunication policy--
Juvenile literature. I. Title.

HE7645.H93 2018   j384.3'3   C2018-903041-0
                                           C2018-903042-9

Library of Congress Cataloging-in-Publication Data

Names: Hyde, Natalie, 1963- author.
Title: Net neutrality / Natalie Hyde.
Description: New York : Crabtree Publishing, [2019] |
Series: Get informed--stay informed |
Includes bibliographical references and index.
Identifiers: LCCN 2018033712 (print) | LCCN 2018036287 (ebook) |
ISBN 9781427121219 (Electronic) |
ISBN 9780778749684 (hardcover) |
ISBN 9780778749721 (pbk.)
Subjects: LCSH: Network neutrality--Juvenile literature.
Classification: LCC HE7645 (ebook) |
LCC HE7645 .H93 2019 (print) | DDC 384.30973--dc23
LC record available at https://lccn.loc.gov/2018033712

Crabtree Publishing Company

www.crabtreebooks.com   1-800-387-7650

Printed in the U.S.A./102018/CG20180810

Published in Canada
Crabtree Publishing
616 Welland Ave.
St. Catharines, ON
L2M 5V6

Published in the United States
Crabtree Publishing
PMB 59051
350 Fifth Avenue, 59th Floor
New York, NY 10118

Published in the United Kingdom
Crabtree Publishing
Maritime House
Basin Road North, Hove
BN41 1WR

Published in Australia
Crabtree Publishing
3 Charles Street
Coburg North
VIC, 3058

CONTENTS

Ready to pay your electricity bill? Which package do you have? Just the kitchen **bundle**? This lets you use electricity for your fridge, microwave, and toaster. That's $50 a month. Do you need a lights package to light your home at night? That's a $20 add-on. Do you have a swimming pool? Maybe you want the outdoor package to fire up a pool heater or pump? Add $15, please.

▲ Using the Internet to play computer games with people all around the world requires high-speed access from your ISP.

▼ Protestors rally for net neutrality in Philadelphia, Pennsylvania, January 2016.

QUESTIONS TO ASK

Within this book are three types of boxes with questions to help your critical thinking about net neutrality. The icons will help you identify them.

THE CENTRAL ISSUES
Learning about the main points of information.

WHAT'S AT STAKE
Helping you determine how the issue will affect you.

ASK YOUR OWN QUESTIONS
Prompts for gaps in your understanding.

FREELY AVAILABLE OR LIMITED ACCESS?

Does the electricity usage system outlined opposite sound ridiculous? Electricity is considered to be a **utility**—a constantly available service provided to run homes and workplaces. You are charged one price for the service and can use the electricity on your property whenever and wherever you like.

Water, sewage, and natural gas are utilities, too. But what about Internet access for your electronic devices? Is that a utility? Or can Internet Service Providers (ISPs) control your access to **data** and websites by charging you for different bundles and also limit the speed of downloading?

WHO IS IN CONTROL?

What ISPs can do is the basis of the **debate** around net neutrality, which is the idea that all information on the Internet can be accessed equally. Is access to the Internet a utility or not and who, if anyone, should be allowed to control it? The outcome of the debate will affect prices, access, and advances in **digital** technology.

Net neutrality is a topic that affects almost everyone, even including people who don't have a computer or Internet access at home. Looking for a new job or home is done online. Public pool schedules, sports team fixtures, road closures, weather alerts, and store coupons are available online. People without Internet access are already at a disadvantage. Restricting or blocking the Internet will affect everyone else, too. This is why the debate over net neutrality is something you should follow and be concerned about.

Everything that happens in **society** changes how you live. The fight over net neutrality is one of those things. Computers and the Internet are everywhere in our lives. Deciding if the Internet should be controlled by governments or businesses will affect how and when you connect with people, ideas, or products. And having the most **current** and **accurate** information is a way to protect yourself from unforeseen influences.

There is no free expression when you have to pay extra to stand on the soap box.

Canadian journalist
Thor Benson

YOU DECIDE

If you don't stay informed, you allow other people to make decisions that affect you. Other people have their own needs and wants. What they decide might be good for their situation, but it won't necessarily be good for yours. By not keeping current, you risk having your rights reversed, or even having **privileges** taken away. If you don't know where you stand on net neutrality, you are in danger of letting businesses make decisions that are good for them, not you.

WHAT'S GOING ON?

Getting informed means understanding the **context** of the topic you are researching. Context is the setting of a topic or event. The context of net neutrality is a time when wireless networks connect millions of people to news information, services, products, and other people.

It is hard to imagine our world without the Internet. It is a vital part of how most of us live, work, and communicate. Understanding the context of the fight over net neutrality allows you to see how far-reaching and damaging changes might be. Gathering information, seeing opposite sides, and checking accuracy are good ways to start. Then you must keep informed.

THE CENTRAL ISSUES

If your access to the Internet is changed or controlled, what parts of your life will be affected and in what ways? Will this have a major impact on your family, friends, and community? Why or why not?

ISP
Internet Service Provider

▲ The first Internet Service Providers were Pegasus Network in Australia in September 1989 and The World in Boston, Massachusetts, in November 1989. **Commercial** ISPs are more in favor of no net neutrality.

◀ Former U.S. Federal Communications **Commission** commissioner Mignon Clyburn talks to protesters. Clyburn was a supporter of net neutrality during her time on the FCC.

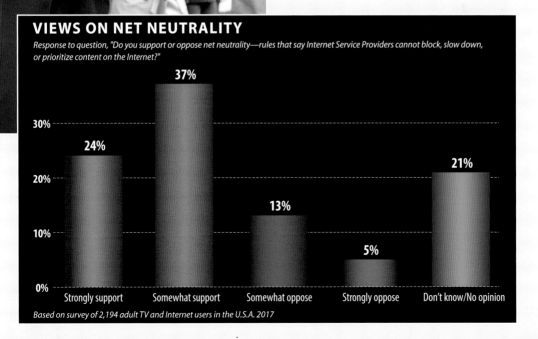

VIEWS ON NET NEUTRALITY

Response to question, "Do you support or oppose net neutrality—rules that say Internet Service Providers cannot block, slow down, or prioritize content on the Internet?"

- Strongly support: 24%
- Somewhat support: 37%
- Somewhat oppose: 13%
- Strongly oppose: 5%
- Don't know/No opinion: 21%

Based on survey of 2,194 adult TV and Internet users in the U.S.A. 2017

With any topic, start by getting **key** background information. For instance, for the fight over net neutrality, read up on the U.S. Telecommunications Act of 1996. Identify the different sides of the issue. For net neutrality, you can research Internet Service Providers and how those organizations work. You can also then read about the Federal Communications Commission (FCC). Don't forget to see how the issue is seen in other countries around the world. The Netherlands was the first European country to make net neutrality law in 2012.

FEDERAL COMMUNICATIONS COMM

LOW RISK • HIGH RISK

WHAT'S AT STAKE?

Why is net neutrality liked by consumers—people who pay for access to the Internet, such as you, your family, and school—but not by Internet Service Providers?

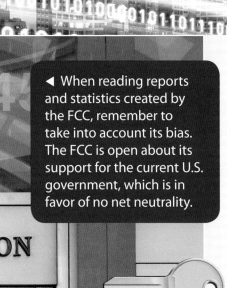

◀ When reading reports and statistics created by the FCC, remember to take into account its bias. The FCC is open about its support for the current U.S. government, which is in favor of no net neutrality.

KEY PLAYERS

The FCC—the Federal Communications Commission—is an agency of the U.S. government. It was created in 1934 to regulate communications by radio, television, wire, satellite, and cable. It is responsible for using and administering communications laws and **regulations**. It is involved in all decisions on net neutrality. Individuals and organizations can submit their views on the issue to the FCC for review and consideration.

TIME AND PLACE

The Time and Place Rule will help you find and judge the most **reliable** information on a topic. This rule states that the closer to the actual event material is created, the more likely it will be accurate, reliable, and **credible.** For the net neutrality debate, some examples of sources are:

- transcripts of hearings on net neutrality
- web films such as *The Internet Must Go*
- interviews with protestors at a rally to keep net neutrality laws
- a magazine article written about the chairperson of the FCC
- a report about the effects of the Open Internet Order in 2010.

It is important to also look up key ISP players in the debate. The main companies affected by net neutrality rules are Deutsche Telekom, Vodafone, or Telefonica in Europe. In the United States search for companies such as Comcast, Charter, AT&T, Verizon, and Sprint. Understand how Facebook, Google, and Netflix use the Internet for their services. They are represented by the Internet Association—an organization that is working to support rules to protect the Internet's future.

You also need to be aware that every piece of information contains the **bias** of its creator, whether intentional or unintentional. Bias is the slant for or against something that people have. Bias seeps into everything. It determines what parts of an event are covered by the **media.** It is important to recognize that bias is present, so you can look behind it in what you read or watch.

Anything that is created to provide information is called source material. Documents, newspapers, photographs, maps, graphs, and interview recordings are all source materials. There are primary, secondary, and tertiary categories of source material (see sidebar on the opposite page). Primary sources are usually considered the most reliable, so when you are getting informed, look for these when you can.

THE VALUE OF THE INTERNET

It is **ironic** that how much information you can find online about net neutrality depends on whether or not you have uncontrolled Internet access and provision. Digital sources are often more current, or up to date, than printed sources because websites can be updated within minutes. Social media sites such as Facebook, Twitter, and blogs, can give you instant insights into people's opinions and viewpoints. Online magazines, newspapers, and news programs can give you details about events relating to your topic. Getting your information from a variety of sources gives you a balanced view of a topic.

START AT THE BEGINNING

To get informed, you first want to know how the topic began. For net neutrality, it would help to learn how the Internet was created and how it worked in the beginning. What laws or regulations were created in the past? What changes have taken place in the meantime? What are the different sides in the debate? Consider reading both primary and secondary sources. Watch news programs or documentaries with footage of protests or government hearings. This will help you understand where the issue is now.

▲ With no net neutrality, it would be difficult to control Internet traffic and content. Providers of computer antivirus software will want to charge more. This might mean some people can't afford to protect their data. Computer viruses would be able to spread more easily around the world.

▶ Internet TV such as YouTube TV and Sony PlayStation Vue were taking viewers away from cable companies and so reducing cable companies' profits. If net neutrality ends, cable companies will be better able to control the access they provide users and cut their costs.

SOURCE MATERIALS

Primary sources are the original creators or owners of information. An example would be the results of an Internet access speed test on your computer.

Secondary sources are reports, analyses, and **interpretations** of the primary sources, for example, a graph created by an ISP for average Internet speeds for their customers.

Tertiary sources are summaries or databases of primary and secondary information. They include Wikipedia articles or entries in encyclopedias.

The Internet came together as a miracle, really. Anyone with a wire can publish; we need to keep it that way.

Barry Diller, U.S. businessman

As you begin to research your topic, you will run across key vocabulary, players, and concepts. Key players are the individuals or groups that form the different sides of the net neutrality debate. By considering all **perspectives**, you can make an informed opinion of your own.

It is **vital** to fully understand the words and phrases that you will see in source material. Look for definitions of technical and jargon terms in a trustworthy dictionary or glossary, either online or in print form. In the debate over net neutrality, you will likely hear about **lobbyists**, the FCC, **broadband** services, ISPs, **legislation**, commission, and many more.

Some of the key concepts you may run across in researching net neutrality are **discrimination**, Internet regulation, and utilities. Understanding how these concepts play a part in this debate will help you grasp the effects the outcome will have on your use of the Internet.

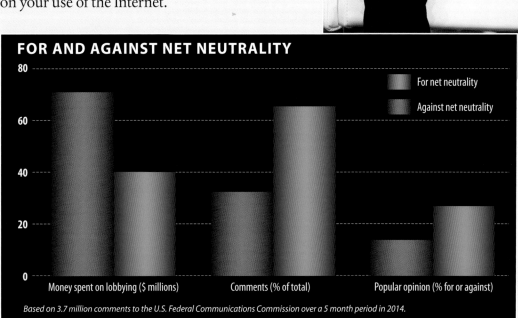

FOR AND AGAINST NET NEUTRALITY

Legend:
- For net neutrality
- Against net neutrality

Y-axis: 0, 20, 40, 60, 80

X-axis categories: Money spent on lobbying ($ millions) | Comments (% of total) | Popular opinion (% for or against)

Based on 3.7 million comments to the U.S. Federal Communications Commission over a 5 month period in 2014.

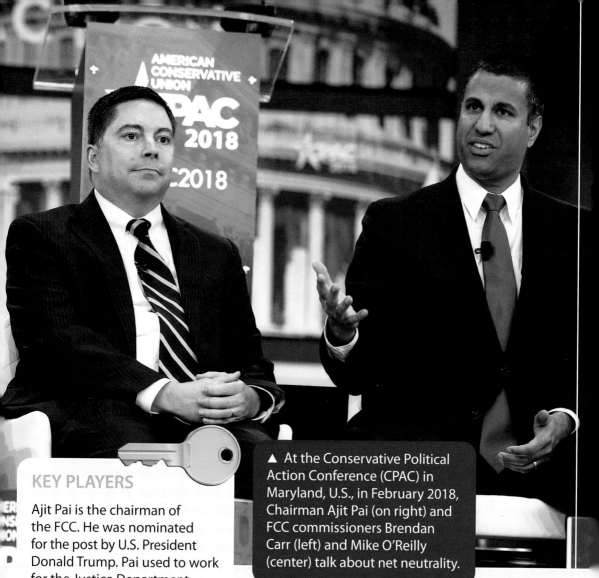

▲ At the Conservative Political Action Conference (CPAC) in Maryland, U.S., in February 2018, Chairman Ajit Pai (on right) and FCC commissioners Brendan Carr (left) and Mike O'Reilly (center) talk about net neutrality.

KEY PLAYERS

Ajit Pai is the chairman of the FCC. He was nominated for the post by U.S. President Donald Trump. Pai used to work for the Justice Department and later was a lawyer for telecommunications company, Verizon. He is against net neutrality. Pai believes that by removing net neutrality, more jobs will be created and new technology will be invented. Pai was awarded the Charlton Heston Courage Under Fire award by the National Rifle Association, for eliminating net neutrality, but he declined a gift from the NRA.

HAVE A LOOK AT THE GRAPHICS

Graphs, charts, and diagrams like the one opposite and on pages 14 and 16 are good visual sources of information. They can present facts and figures in creative and inventive ways. But they, too, can show bias. An ISP might highlight different volumes of data for competing websites so it can charge more for hosting each one. A net neutrality protest group might show how the bigger a company is, the more it can **sway** the government to do what it wants.

WHAT IS NET NEUTRALITY?

Net neutrality is the idea that Internet Service Providers (ISPs) have to treat all data on the Internet equally. That means when customers pay their ISP for Internet access, the whole network is available to them. People can access small websites such as a local apple orchard as easily as a large website such as YouTube. ISPs also have the same download speed for all websites. Countries such as Canada, Japan, and Russia, and all the countries of the **European Union** have laws supporting net neutrality.

> "(Net neutrality is) the idea that all content on the Internet should remain equally accessible, that Internet service providers should not be able to choose which websites load faster than others or even block certain sites."
>
> Michel Martin, host National Public Radio

FLOW OF INFORMATION—WITH AND WITHOUT NET NEUTRALITY

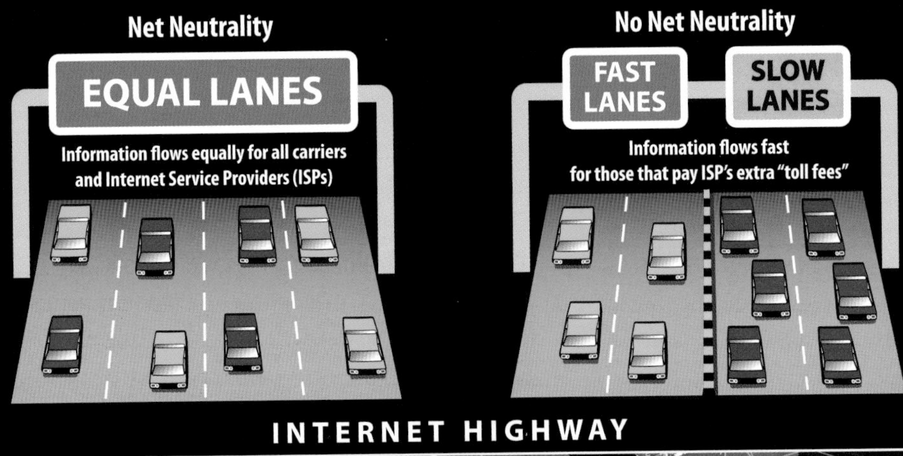

Net Neutrality

EQUAL LANES

Information flows equally for all carriers and Internet Service Providers (ISPs)

No Net Neutrality

FAST LANES **SLOW LANES**

Information flows fast for those that pay ISP's extra "toll fees"

INTERNET HIGHWAY

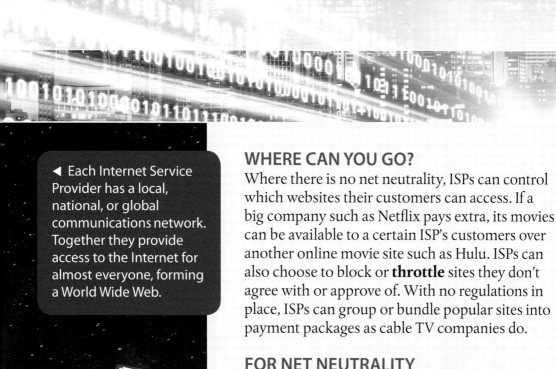

ASK YOUR OWN QUESTIONS

To have a complete picture of a story or event, an article or report should contain the answers to 5 Ws and an H.
• Who was involved?
• What happened?
• When did it take place?
• Where did it take place?
• Why did that happen?
• How did it happen?
Look for these details to make sure what you are reading is giving you a story without holes in it.

WHERE CAN YOU GO?

Where there is no net neutrality, ISPs can control which websites their customers can access. If a big company such as Netflix pays extra, its movies can be available to a certain ISP's customers over another online movie site such as Hulu. ISPs can also choose to block or **throttle** sites they don't agree with or approve of. With no regulations in place, ISPs can group or bundle popular sites into payment packages as cable TV companies do.

FOR NET NEUTRALITY

People in favor of net neutrality say that these laws protect their right to see and visit all sites, no matter how big or small they are or what content they have. They say that without this rule, people with a lower income might not be able to afford more popular sites because of package pricing. They worry that ISPs can **manipulate** what people see and hear. This can lead to swaying public opinion about a topic by not allowing them access to all information.

AGAINST NET NEUTRALITY

People who want net neutrality ended say that ISPs should be able to control how they deliver content, including freedom to speed up Internet access to those who wish to pay more. They say ISPs should also be able to charge more to companies that use a lot of **bandwidth**, such as video streaming. This will leave them more money to invest in new technology. It will also give them the cash to bring Internet services to remote areas.

Learning the background of your topic, including its history, will help you see changes that have already happened. It will also let you imagine what changes might happen in the future. Studying what the Internet is, how it began, and how it now works is vital for understanding how net neutrality affects it.

The Internet had its roots with the Advanced Research Projects Agency (ARPA). ARPA created the first computer network using four huge computers. They called the network ARPANET. Next, they looked into ways to connect their network to the **packet radio** network (PRNET). It connects computers through radio waves instead of phone lines. When they were able to connect these two networks to a third, they called it "Inter-networking." More networks joined. In 1990, Tim Berners-Lee developed a way to make **navigating** these networks simpler. It became known as the World Wide Web.

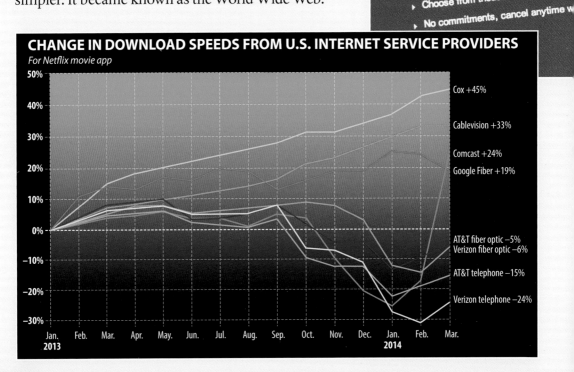

CHANGE IN DOWNLOAD SPEEDS FROM U.S. INTERNET SERVICE PROVIDERS

For Netflix movie app

Cox +45%
Cablevision +33%
Comcast +24%
Google Fiber +19%
AT&T fiber optic −5%
Verizon fiber optic −6%
AT&T telephone −15%
Verizon telephone −24%

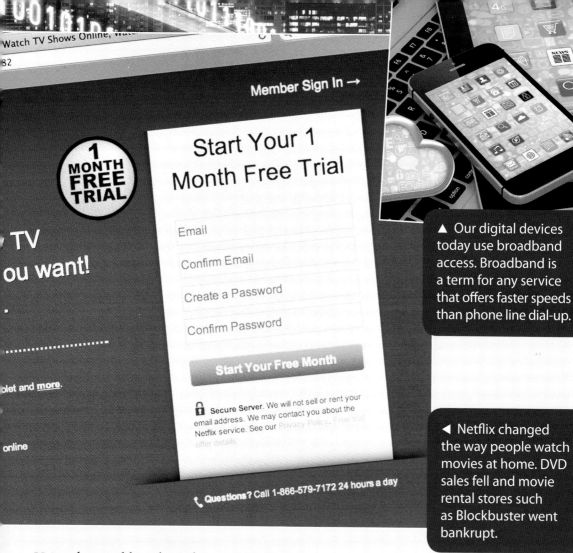

Watch TV Shows Online, ...

82

Member Sign In →

1 MONTH FREE TRIAL

Start Your 1 Month Free Trial

TV
ou want!

Email

Confirm Email

Create a Password

Confirm Password

Start Your Free Month

🔒 **Secure Server.** We will not sell or rent your email address. We may contact you about the Netflix service. See our Privacy Policy. Free trial offer details.

📞 Questions? Call 1-866-579-7172 24 hours a day

plet and **more**.

online

▲ Our digital devices today use broadband access. Broadband is a term for any service that offers faster speeds than phone line dial-up.

◄ Netflix changed the way people watch movies at home. DVD sales fell and movie rental stores such as Blockbuster went bankrupt.

Using the World Wide Web, universities and businesses began to connect to the Internet. Soon the Internet was being used to buy and sell products and services.

A NETWORK OF NETWORKS

Today, the Internet is so much more complex. It connects computers, smartphones, tablets, satellites, and many more gadgets. When you connect to the Internet, you join a network. This is your Internet Service Provider, or ISP. The ISP may then connect to a larger network. You can think of the Internet as a network of networks.

THE CENTRAL ISSUES

Do you think home users should pay the same for Internet access as large businesses? Should nonprofits pay the same as schools and universities?

In 1970, all Internet traffic flowed over phone lines. AT&T, a huge telephone company, controlled these lines. This meant it controlled the Internet. The phone company wanted to treat the Internet like it treated its phone service. It charged extra to customers depending on what they used the phone for. Long distance calls cost extra. A second line to your home cost extra. A business line cost extra. Call display, call forwarding, and an answering service cost extra.

The creators of programs that made the Internet work efficiently designed it so that all applications would be available to everyone. They called it the "open Internet." The FCC agreed. It set the first regulations to allow Internet users to determine how to use the Internet. This could include watching movies, buying or selling items, searching for information, sending e-mails, and making telephone and video calls. These rules worked to keep the control in the hands of users. They were the first net neutrality regulations.

BUYING AND SELLING

But new technology brought changes. Data can now be sent over other media such as cable, **fiber optics**, and satellites. Computers were working faster and the Internet was growing. Each year, more business is done via the Internet. People order flowers, book concert tickets, and hire a plumber without leaving their homes. Stores are feeling the effects. They are losing money. They are looking for ways to make up for their lost **profits.** One way is to find new charges for customers using the Internet. But the net neutrality rules make this impossible. So companies lobbied the FCC to get rid of the rules.

KEY PLAYERS

Internet Service Providers, or ISPs, provide access to the Internet for individuals, organizations, and businesses. Some of the largest ISPs in the United States are Comcast, AT&T, Time Warner, and Verizon. In Canada, the largest ISPs are Bell, Rogers, and Shaw. ISPs are against net neutrality. They want to have control over what customers access on the Internet and how they do it, to keep making money.

ISPs should not be able to engage in any sort of [trickery] that limits or manipulates the choices you make online. "

John Oliver, TV show host

▲ Regulations need to grow and change along with new technology such as these 3D TVs.

◀ France's ISP, OVH, plans to expand its business into North America. It believes it can offer customers more secure service at a cheaper price.

THE CENTRAL ISSUES

Are the concerns the FCC had when the Internet began similar to concerns over net neutrality today?

4 INFORMATION LITERACY

It is important to remember that every topic or debate you may research has more than one point of view. The needs and wants of one person or business are not the same as the needs and wants of someone else. When you want to get an accurate understanding of an issue, you need to listen to all sides. This will give you a balanced view and allow you to have an informed opinion on the subject.

LOW RISK   HIGH RISK

WHAT'S AT STAKE?

If the government only hears the side of Internet providers and big business, how will that affect its decision making? How can ordinary users make their voices heard?

> " Net neutrality touches some very sensitive nerves on both sides of the debate…It goes fundamentally to the heart of what the Internet is and what its role is in our society. "
>
> Kevin Werbach, Professor of Legal Studies and Business Ethics, University of Pennsylvania

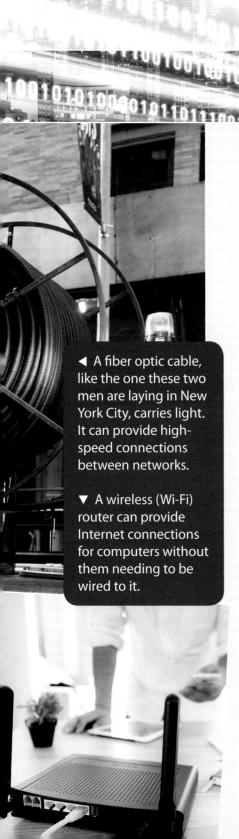

◀ A fiber optic cable, like the one these two men are laying in New York City, carries light. It can provide high-speed connections between networks.

▼ A wireless (Wi-Fi) router can provide Internet connections for computers without them needing to be wired to it.

GOVERNMENT INVOLVEMENT

Governments are supposed to look at an issue from the point of view of what is good for society and all its **citizens**. In the net neutrality debate, governments have been debating how Internet service should be labeled. Some services, such as electricity, water, and sewage, are called public utilities. These are considered everyday, necessary services run by organizations for public use. Each country may have utility companies that are nationalized—run by the government—or run by independent organizations, or a mix of the two. But they follow the same service guidelines.

WHAT SERVICE IS REQUIRED?

If Internet service is labeled a public utility, this will change how much control ISPs have over what they provide and what they charge. ISPs will not be able to restrict access or charge more for separate services. It will also mean that the FCC or other government bodies will have more control over how and where new **infrastructure**, such as new cables or satellites, goes to provide Internet connections.

But you can look at this debate from other viewpoints. ISPs are independent companies that need to make money to pay employees and buy new machines. They want rules that will allow them to be profitable. Customers need ways to access the information they need quickly and easily. They also want to be able to use their computer the way it serves their family best. That can be for banking, shopping, or entertainment.

INTERNET PACKAGES
—LIFE WITHOUT NET NEUTRALITY

PACK 1 **$5** *monthly*

PACK 2 **$20** *monthly*

UNLIMITED **$100** *monthly* **Access to Everything**

▼ Online shopping sales are growing every year. In 2017 more than 2.3 billion dollars were spent around the world buying products and services using the Internet.

HOME | BRAND |

50%

DESIGNER'S

SHO

USE CODE FIFTYOFF

BRANDS

PRE

1234 56

KEY PLAYERS

Craig Aaron is executive director of Free Press, a group fighting for net neutrality rules. He believes that an open Internet is a powerful tool to bring about changes in society. He also believes that Internet access is vital for society to communicate, connect, and organize.

WHAT'S AT STAKE?

LOW RISK   HIGH RISK

If net neutrality is removed, will you have to pay extra for your Snapchat and Pinterest accounts?

If net neutrality rules are ended, then home users will face many changes. Their ISP may begin charging companies to be recommended or have access to their customers. This means customers may not be able to visit or use all the websites they do now. Perhaps their ISP will allow YouTube but not Netflix. Maybe only *CNN* or *Global News* sites will appear, and not the *BBC* news or local stations. This will affect what stories or viewpoints you will be able to read or hear. This means often you will not get a balanced view on a subject.

Without net neutrality, home users might face having to buy their Internet access in packages like cable TV. For one price, an ISP might offer some basic websites such as news and sports. For more money, perhaps you can have a **movie-streaming** site. For another add-on, you can use the Internet as your phone or for video calling.

CASH CRUNCH

For some people, the extra fees might mean they can no longer afford the access they used to have. They will be at a disadvantage in finding jobs online, or finding the best price on products. They will likely also not be as well informed on a subject, which may affect how they vote in elections or what health choices they make.

ISPs say the extra money will allow them to improve services. They say they will be able to bring Internet service to more remote areas. This will increase the number of people overall who can use the Internet. They also intend to lay more fiber optic cables, which will increase Internet speeds for **existing** customers (see graph on page 25). Even people living in countries like Canada that have net neutrality laws might be affected. Canadian customers may have to pay to access certain US markets. The whole Internet world will change.

◄ Very few people are buying music CDs. More than 30 million people stream their music over the Internet from their ISP.

Billions of dollars in business is done over the Internet. Companies both large and small rely on reaching customers across the country and around the globe to stay profitable. And more people shop online than ever before. In the United States, about 96 percent of the population has shopped online. In Canada, online shopping sales numbers are expected to reach $39 billion a year. Most people prefer shopping online because it saves them time. They can also shop any time of the day or night and they can avoid crowds and long line-ups at the checkout. Forty-nine percent of people feel that shopping online is more convenient than shopping in person. Their biggest complaint? Paying for **shipping**.

WHAT'S AT STAKE?

If ISPs charge higher fees or place restrictions on businesses, how will that affect your ability to support local businesses? How might this affect your community?

► Shoes and other items are readied for resale at an online business's warehouse in Salt Lake City, Utah.

▼ Amazon warehouses, like this one in Rheinberg, Germany, are huge. They have hundreds of employees who process about 35 orders per second!

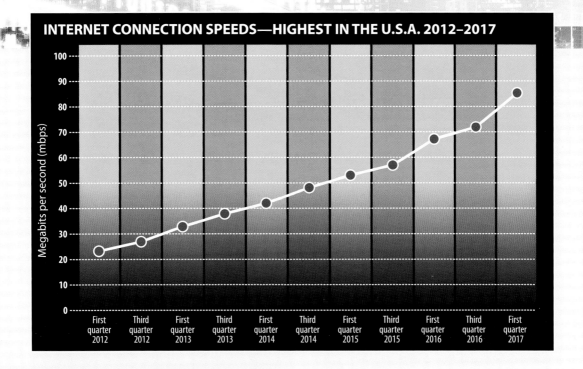

INTERNET CONNECTION SPEEDS—HIGHEST IN THE U.S.A. 2012–2017

Y-axis: Megabits per second (mbps), 0 to 100

X-axis: First quarter 2012, Third quarter 2012, First quarter 2013, Third quarter 2013, First quarter 2014, Third quarter 2014, First quarter 2015, Third quarter 2015, First quarter 2016, Third quarter 2016, First quarter 2017

> *People want to connect to a product, be it through enhanced imagery, recommendations, reviews, blogs, social media, etc.*
>
> Genevieve Kunst, Director of POPSUGAR, a fashion search engine

BREAKING IN

If there is no net neutrality, experts believe that ISPs will begin charging online businesses extra to be included in their access packages. This will not be a problem for huge companies who are already doing well. But small businesses and new businesses will face difficulties. They may not have the **budgets** to pay large fees to have their businesses included. Or they may only be able to pay one or two Internet Service Providers, but not all of them. This means they will not be able to reach as many customers or make as many sales. New companies trying to break into a market will find it impossible to find new customers. This also means that customers may find they have less choice when looking for an item or for an essential service.

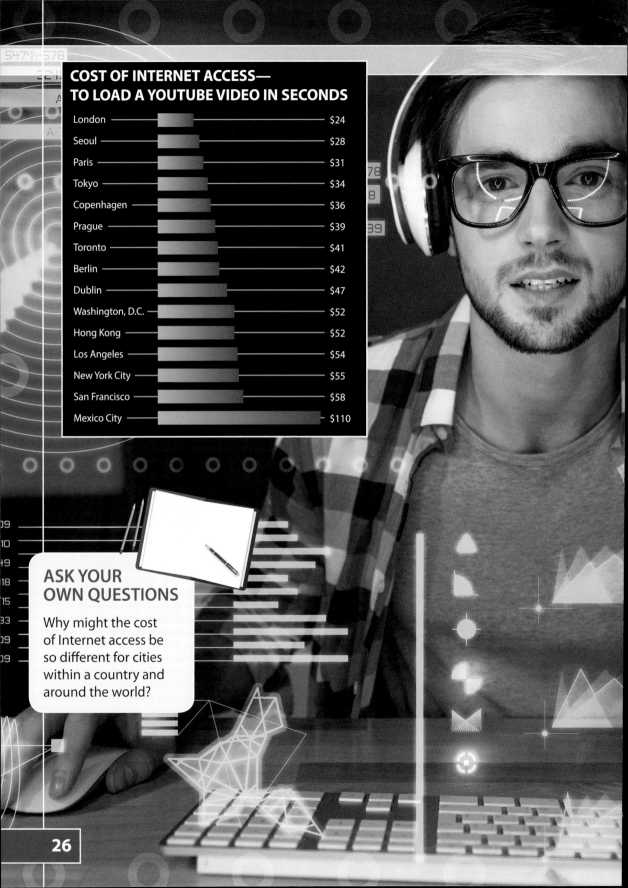

COST OF INTERNET ACCESS—
TO LOAD A YOUTUBE VIDEO IN SECONDS

London	$24
Seoul	$28
Paris	$31
Tokyo	$34
Copenhagen	$36
Prague	$39
Toronto	$41
Berlin	$42
Dublin	$47
Washington, D.C.	$52
Hong Kong	$52
Los Angeles	$54
New York City	$55
San Francisco	$58
Mexico City	$110

ASK YOUR OWN QUESTIONS

Why might the cost of Internet access be so different for cities within a country and around the world?

26

◄ As new technology—such as this transparent screen—is developed, Internet speeds and services will need to keep up.

"
Your ability to access a website depends on your desire to access the website and not the deals that the intermediaries have made with each other.
"

Cindy Cohn, American Civil Liberties Attorney specializing in Internet law

Part of the argument made by ISPs against net neutrality is that they don't have the money or any reason to upgrade under that system. They say, in order to pay for new technology, they need more freedom. Without restrictions, ISPs say they will improve networks and bring Internet services to rural areas. With a new pricing system, ISPs have told the FCC they will make more money. They will take that money and invest in infrastructure such as new towers and cables. This will lead to more jobs and broadband Internet access for more people.

A STEADY AND FREE SERVICE

Some of those new technologies include solar-powered **drones**. These drones would beam Internet service back down to Earth. Facebook owner Mark Zuckerberg has developed a drone called *Aquila* and its test flights have been successful. Drones like *Aquila* would fly in a 60-mile- (97-km) wide circle above the clouds. The Sun would provide all the energy, and Internet connections would be steady and free. Google has been working on the idea of using large balloons to provide Internet service to very remote areas. Another company in France is using LED lights to make Wi-Fi 100 times faster.

NO NEED TO CHANGE

Some people argue that ISPs are not going to change how they invest without net neutrality laws. They are already improving their systems to stay ahead of their competitors. They believe that the extra money ISPs may make by bundling services will not change what they were going to do. The new inventions are not being developed by ISP companies, but by small design companies. They argue that ISPs would be buying and using the new technology anyway.

27

The Internet has been extremely important in keeping the world connected. People in different countries, with different cultures and languages, can share ideas and opinions. Before the Internet, news of world events took hours or even days to reach other parts of the planet. This affected the time it took for help to come for natural disasters or human tragedies.

The Internet has also been vital in times of conflict. During the Arab Spring **uprising** in Egypt in 2011, messages were spread across the country and rallies set up online. The government tried to shut down people's access to the Internet to stop the protests. People found ways to get around the obstacles to continue connecting with one another. The Internet proved to be a powerful way for the public to organize and be heard.

LOSS OF KNOWLEDGE

This is the type of thing some people fear with ISPs being able to control which sites they allow people to access and which they will not. A company that supports one political party over another might refuse to allow websites that criticize politicians. ISPs that have members who do not support equal rights for all might refuse to allow websites that discuss women's rights or **LGBTQ** events. By trying to restrict what people see, hear, or understand, ISPs could increase hate, fear, and the loss of rights.

Canada still has net neutrality regulations. However, repealing those rules in other countries can affect how open the Internet might be for Canadians. People question whether Canadian companies will have to pay extra to access certain U.S. markets, harming their success.

THE CENTRAL ISSUES

How big a role does the Internet play in business? Is it equally important to large and small businesses? Why or why not? Which of the bundles shown in the graphic above would all businesses need?

PAYING MORE FOR EXTRA DATA—NO NET NEUTRALITY

$4.99 monthly — Messaging

$4.99 monthly — Social

$4.99 monthly — Video

$4.99 monthly — Music

$4.99 monthly — Email & Cloud

Basic Access

◄ In April 2018, Russians gathered in Moscow to demand Internet freedom. The government was blocking popular sites that were criticizing the country's leaders.

РУКИ ПРОЧЬ ОТ ИНТЕРНЕТА

5 WHERE THINGS STAND

The world is changing all the time. **Issues** change, too. New information, new players, new ideas, and new technology can affect how we view a topic. Another problem you need to be aware of is misinformation.

INFOWARS

RADIO SHOW   NEWS   VIDEOS   STORE   TOP STORIES   BREAKING NEWS

THE RUSSIAN-TRUMP CONSPIRACY IS FAKE NEWS

FEATURED STORIES   ALL NEWS

WHAT'S AT STAKE?

Why is it vital to have accurate information? Who might gain from spreading false information?

ORDER TODAY

NO $9. SILVER B COLLOIDA

STOREWIDE FREE

GET IT FOR XMAS   BUY

TODAY ON THE ALEX JONES

n this Tuesday, Dec. 13 transmission of the Ale over the establishment's plan to use Russia as revent Trump from being inaugurated. **Roger**

◀ Fake news is based on opinions and lies. Real news is always backed up with facts that can be confirmed or verified by an **objective** source.

RELIABLE INFORMATION

Misinformation is data that is misleading, misunderstood, or just plain wrong. The problem is that misinformation spreads as quickly or even quicker than the truth. Why? Sometimes it is because we have an idea in our mind already about a topic. When we read something that tells us the opposite, we don't want to change our minds. It is also hard to question something when all our family and friends say it must be true.

So how do you get to the truth? You need to look at facts, not opinions. Check your sources. If they have something to gain by convincing you of their viewpoint, be cautious. Big businesses and corporations will always want to keep the money rolling in. The most reliable facts come from organizations that will not profit from the debate going one way or another. Statistics Canada and U.S. Data and Statistics are good places to start.

GET TO THE TRUTH

If you let yourself be swayed by people with strong opinions that can't be backed up with solid facts, you are not truly well informed. If you just accept the first things you read on the Internet, you are not going to get to the truth. If you read up on a subject and then don't see how the topic is changing, you will not stay informed. Don't be afraid to ask questions and dig deeper.

The debate about net neutrality is ongoing. You will read claims, and counterclaims, from governments, ISPs, and consumer groups about what is best. You must make up your own mind.

TEST CASES AND CONTROVERSIES

Just because a country supports net neutrality now, doesn't mean the regulations can't be overturned in the future. Countries that have no protection for a free and open Internet today, may bring it back. This might also happen if a different political party is voted in as the ruling party. The issue is always changing.

THE CANADIAN GOVERNMENT STEPS IN

In Canada, the Canadian Radio-television and Telecommunications Commission (CRTC) is in charge of Internet regulations. The CRTC supports strict net neutrality. It stepped in when some ISPs were not providing equal services to all websites. One company allowed customers to view its mobile television for free while charging for other websites or apps. The CRTC made them stop. It has also created rules around pricing. This way, everyone has choice and the chance to exchange ideas freely. But even with net neutrality rules, the CRTC has to closely watch ISP companies.

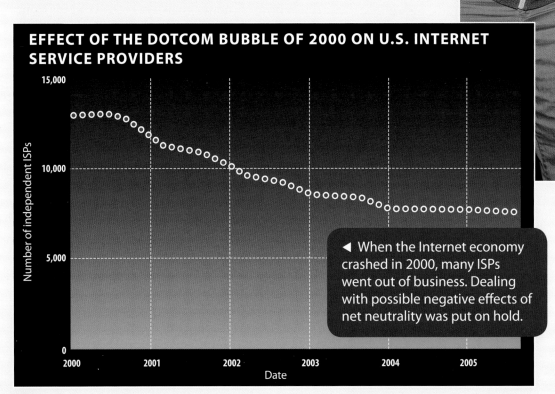

EFFECT OF THE DOTCOM BUBBLE OF 2000 ON U.S. INTERNET SERVICE PROVIDERS

◀ When the Internet economy crashed in 2000, many ISPs went out of business. Dealing with possible negative effects of net neutrality was put on hold.

CONGRESS:

PLEASE #STOPTHEFCC FROM KILLING NET NEUTRALITY. NO CENSORSHIP, THROTTLING, OR EXTRA FEES ONLINE.

BATTLEFORTHENET.COM

#STOPTHEFCC

◀ Demonstrators protest outside of the ISP Verizon's offices in Massachusetts. Many people say they will continue fighting until net neutrality rules are put back in place. Verizon is one of the big ISPs that survived the crash of the Internet industry when big changes happened too fast.

WHAT HAPPENS NEXT

In the United States, net neutrality rules have been **repealed**. Experts are waiting to see what will happen. ISPs insist that the Internet was fair and open before the Open Internet Rule. They feel that the regulations were unnecessary. But in August 2008, the ISP Comcast was ordered by the FCC to stop slowing down traffic from the company BitTorrent. BitTorrent is a video- and music-sharing site. Without net neutrality rules in place, Comcast could again restrict traffic.

SEARCH TIPS

There are search tools for finding an expert on a certain topic. Type the subject into the search bar. This will help you find experts doing up-to-date research.

Google Scholar:
https://scholar.google.ca

Microsoft Academic Search:
https://academic.microsoft.com

Expertise Finder:
http://expertisefinder.com

Myths are stories that have been repeated so often, people start to believe them. They can be dangerous because people stop checking to see if the facts are true. If they are convinced there is no problem, they won't act to fix it. Some of the most common net neutrality myths are:

Most *innovation* on the Internet happened before 2005 net neutrality laws.
The Internet Association showed that ISPs actually increased **investments** after net neutrality laws. Important new technologies and systems were developed. Experts say this is because large companies could not use their money and power to shut down new, smaller start-ups. These smaller companies often brought new ways of doing things online.

Net neutrality laws are unnecessary. The Internet was "free and open" before they were introduced.
The fact is that ISPs have a history of trying to block or control what content they provide. Even with net neutrality laws in place, there have been situations of discrimination. Time Warner's AOL was blocking certain e-mails that mentioned the protest to stop AOL's idea of pay-to-send e-mails. In Canada, Telus blocked striking union workers from accessing a website run by their union.

Network operators are protecting customers.
Like any company, ISPs are in business to make money. Their decisions are based on creating profit to keep their doors open and their employees paid. To do this, they need to beat out their competition and stop new businesses from taking their customers. Most ISPs have already shown that they cannot regulate themselves.

WHAT'S AT STAKE?

Why are people so easily misled on the Internet? Why are myths more easily spread online than on TV, on radio, or in newpapers?

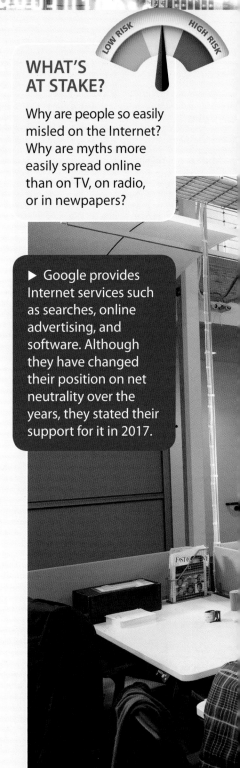

▶ Google provides Internet services such as searches, online advertising, and software. Although they have changed their position on net neutrality over the years, they stated their support for it in 2017.

◀ Some young adults use the Internet in all parts of their lives—online learning, job searches, communication, entertainment, and even dating.

" *The FCC's net neutrality rules are working well for consumers, and we're disappointed in the proposal released today.* "

Google statement after FCC proposed getting rid of net neutrality rules

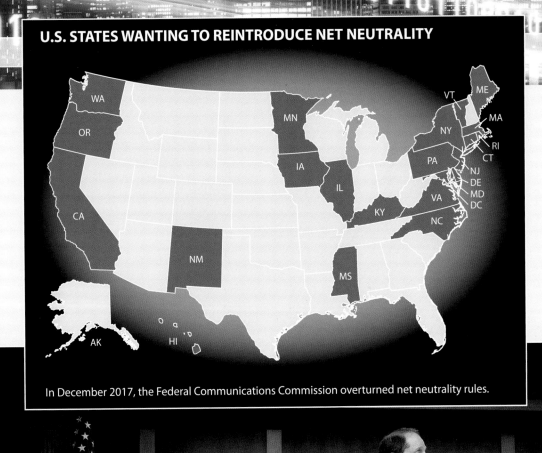

U.S. STATES WANTING TO REINTRODUCE NET NEUTRALITY

In December 2017, the Federal Communications Commission overturned net neutrality rules.

▶ Senator Ron Wyden speaks at a press conference for a review to reverse the FCC's decision.

C approves controversial
t neutrality' rules

▲ The FCC stated that most of the public input about net neutrality was spam and the rest was in favor of scrapping it. A study paid for by the broadband industry said that 98.5 percent of non-spam comments on the FCC website supported keeping net neutrality rules.

WHAT'S AT STAKE?

Will new pricing and blocked access affect minorities more than other groups in society? Why? Could this turn into a racial issue? How?

In Canada, polls show that almost 90 percent of Canadians are for some form of net neutrality laws. Many people are concerned that the change in the United States (see map opposite) will affect their costs in the future. So far, the CRTC has had the support of all parties in the government.

In the United States, the debate over net neutrality changes as the government has changed. The FCC is made up of members nominated by the political party in power. This means its position tends to change, depending on which party is the majority. The repeal, or rejection, of the net neutrality rules in the United States took effect on June 11, 2018.

WHO'S IN CHARGE

The FCC is stepping back, but says there will still be an agency to watch over the Internet. The Federal Trade Commission (FTC) will take over **policing** complaints. But net neutrality supporters say this isn't good enough. The FTC already oversees all other types of customer complaints. People worry that it is already too busy to properly watch over Internet problems. The FTC also does not have the power to make rules, only to **enforce** what is already law. This is a problem with the Internet, where the rules were just removed.

So what is happening now? While there is no federal law anymore, some states are taking matters into their own hands. More than half the states have begun the process to create new state laws that will protect net neutrality. Some states have sued the FCC. Others are doing nothing. This patchwork of different rules will make it difficult for an ISP company that operates in many or all states.

The net neutrality debate has been going on in other countries, as well. To get informed, it is important to remember to look outside your own country. Looking at how others are succeeding or failing with an issue is a good source of information of what works and what doesn't.

DIFFERENT APPROACHES

Around the world, different countries and continents have approached net neutrality laws in different ways. Brazil does not have net neutrality laws. It does have some regulations that allow ISPs to slow Internet traffic only for very specific reasons. But it does nothing to stop ISP companies that openly ignore these rules.

The European Union has approved strong rules to support net neutrality. The rules allow traffic restrictions only in case of emergency or for security reasons. India has also very strict rules. These countries are serious about protecting customers' rights to access whatever content they want for whatever use they want. Portugal does not allow ISPs to slow or block data, but ISPs are allowed to bundle apps to charge different prices.

Australia does not have net neutrality laws, but does have regulations around blocking and slowing traffic. The difference in Australia is that they have more than 60 ISPs, so the Internet is not controlled by only one or two huge corporations. This means ISPs do not have the power to restrict access without losing customers.

Half of the population in the United States has only one choice for an ISP in their area, and only 20 percent has two choices. Almost 30 percent of people in the United States have no high-speed Internet service.

▼ As of 2017, South Korea has the fastest average Internet connection. It is four times faster than the world average. The chart opposite compares Internet download speeds in different countries.

The Internet is the most valuable invention of the 20th century, and we should all be fighting to keep it free.

Hadi Ghaemi, Executive Director of the Center for Human Rights in Iran

BROADBAND INTERNET DOWNLOAD SPEEDS, APRIL 2018
In megabits per second

Country	Speed
Singapore	174.94
Iceland	162.43
Hong Kong	141.05
South Korea	110.10
Romania	107.01
Hungary	94.72
Sweden	93.69
Switzerland	93.07
United States	91.46
Macau	90.29
Netherlands	83.24
Norway	82.22
Denmark	81.84
Canada	80.08
Japan	76.31
China	75.43
Spain	75.20
New Zealand	74.22

341730 1

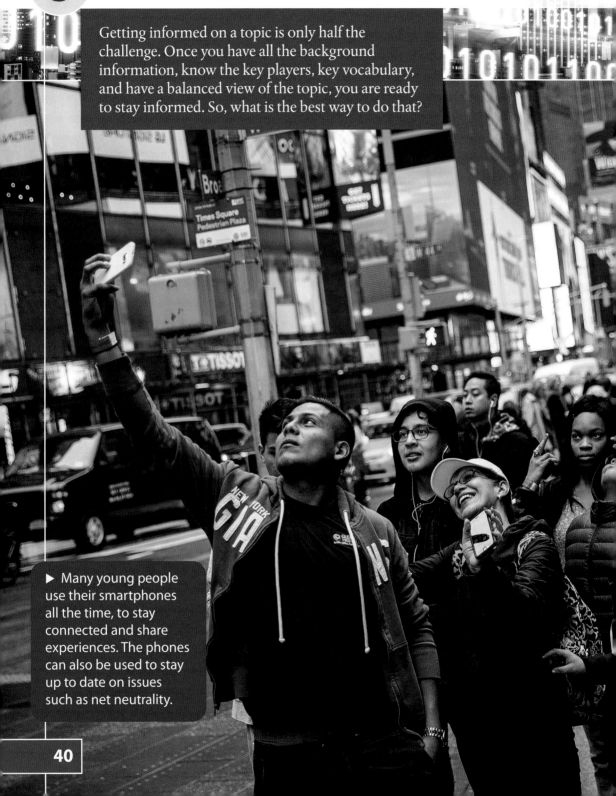

6 KEEPING UP TO DATE

Getting informed on a topic is only half the challenge. Once you have all the background information, know the key players, key vocabulary, and have a balanced view of the topic, you are ready to stay informed. So, what is the best way to do that?

▶ Many young people use their smartphones all the time, to stay connected and share experiences. The phones can also be used to stay up to date on issues such as net neutrality.

WHAT IS YOUR NEWS DIET?

It's a good idea to make a list of source materials for your **news diet**. Sources such as newspapers and magazine articles can be helpful. However, because it takes time to print and **distribute** them, they are not always up to date. TV or online news sites usually have current news.

Take the time to check that your sources are reliable. Do this by researching who or what organization is providing the information. Are they trying to convince you to take sides? Are they selling something? Look behind the scenes to identify any bias their content may have. Add sites that will give you information from other countries and organizations.

Among key sources you might review are:
- American Civil Liberties Union (ACLU), which tries to preserve people's rights and liberties
- Newspapers and magazines such as *Newsweek, The Economist,* and *The New York Times*
- TV news from private and public networks.

Once you have a list of reliable sources, set up ways to get information as it comes in. Google alerts can notify you if a certain word or phrase is posted online. If you need help to do this, go to www.google.com/alerts. There are also sites that will collect daily news for you in one easy list. You can use them on your computer or smartphone. There are several different apps that will let you browse blogs, news sites, **podcasts,** and magazines. Flipboard, Feedly, and Google Play Newsstand are just some of these apps.

Don't forget to fact check! Even if you have identified bias and checked the source, everyone makes mistakes. Even reliable sites can pass along incorrect details by accident. Sites with a good **reputation** will list their sources at the end of an article or under pictures. (Sources used for this book are listed on page 46.) Follow the trail to verify that what has been reported is true. Use statistics sites to double-check numbers and percentages.

Read articles or blogs by experts on a subject. Don't be afraid to ask them questions if you don't understand something. As long as you ask politely and are respectful of how busy they are, most experts are happy to share their knowledge. Getting information from someone studying a topic means you will gain reliable, accurate facts.

SPEAKING UP

The fight over net neutrality is not over. In countries such as Canada that have strict rules in place, you can make sure they do not get eroded. In countries that are facing changes, such as the United States, you can voice your opinion. Keeping up to date lets you know what events or protests are happening. You can decide to call your government representative. You can comment on a company's website. You can check with your own ISP to see what it is saying or promising. Information helps you get involved.

Be an informed, educated member of your community. This will not only help society treat people in a fair and just manner, but you will also make better choices for yourself. Armed with accurate information, you will be able to help steer your world, big or small, to a better future.

WHAT'S AT STAKE?

With reference to the graph opposite, what new developments in net neutrality might spark more surges in comments to the FCC?

SEARCH TIPS

Use quotation marks around a phrase to search for that exact combination of words (for example, "net neutrality").

Use a colon and an extension to search a specific site (for example, Broadband:.gov for all government website mention of the system).

Use the word Define and a colon to search for word definitions (for example, Define: infrastructure).

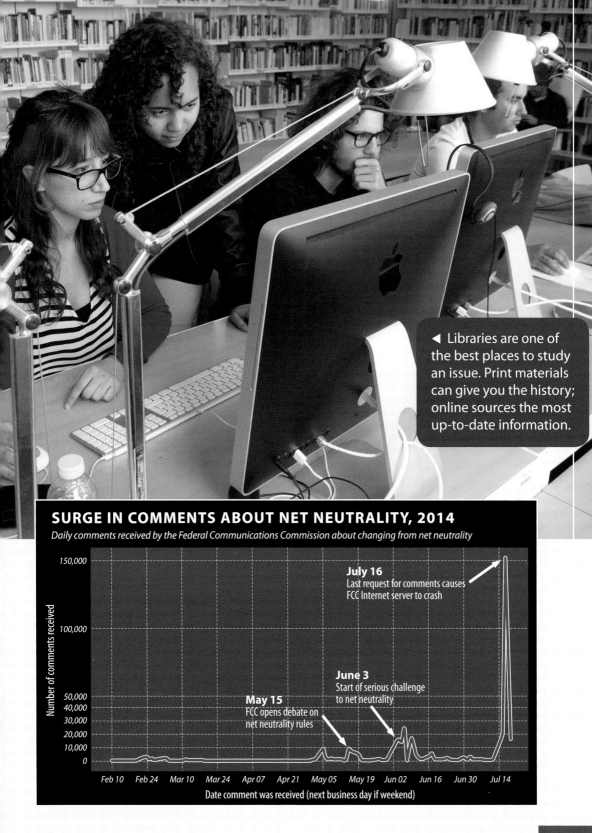

◀ Libraries are one of the best places to study an issue. Print materials can give you the history; online sources the most up-to-date information.

SURGE IN COMMENTS ABOUT NET NEUTRALITY, 2014

Daily comments received by the Federal Communications Commission about changing from net neutrality

July 16
Last request for comments causes FCC Internet server to crash

June 3
Start of serious challenge to net neutrality

May 15
FCC opens debate on net neutrality rules

Number of comments received

150,000
100,000
50,000
40,000
30,000
20,000
10,000
0

Feb 10   Feb 24   Mar 10   Mar 24   Apr 07   Apr 21   May 05   May 19   Jun 02   Jun 16   Jun 30   Jul 14

Date comment was received (next business day if weekend)

GLOSSARY

accurate Correct in all details

analyzing Studying something carefully

bandwidth The amount of information that can be sent along a channel

bias Prejudice in favor for or against something or someone

broadband A way to send digital messages quickly

budget The amount of money you can spend on a project

bundle To collect things together; a group of things

citizens The people belonging legally to a country

commercial Related to buying or selling things

commission A group of people responsible for something

context The circumstances or situation surrounding something

credible Able to be trusted or believed

current Happening now

data Internet access through a smartphone

debate A formal discussion

dependable Trustworthy

digital Using technology like satellites and fiber optics

discrimination Unjustly treating a person or group of people differently

distribute Give out

drones Aircraft with no pilot or crew

enforce Make people obey the law

European Union 28 countries in Europe that operate as one unit for trade

evaluate Work out the importance or worth

existing Already in place

fiber optics Thin fibers with a glass core to transmit light signals

infrastructure The material structures needed for something to work

innovation New ideas

interpretations Explanations or meanings of things written or said

investments Money spent expecting to get more back in the future

ironic Happening the opposite of what you expected

issues Important topics for debate

key Very important

legislation Law-making

LGBTQ Stands for: lesbian, gay, bisexual, transgender, and queer or questioning

lobbyists People working to sway the decisions of politicians

manipulate Control for your own gain

media Methods of mass communication such as television and radio

movie streaming Using the Internet to watch videos

navigating Finding a route

news diet The sources you use to get your news

objective Without bias; a balanced viewpoint

packet radio Broadcasting using radio signals carrying packets of data

perspectives Viewpoints, outlooks

podcasts Spoken information made available on the Internet

policing Making people follow the law

privileges Special rights to do things

profits Money earned from selling goods or services such as Internet access

regulations Rules

reliable Always good quality

repealed Cancelled

reputation What others think of a person or company

shipping Transporting goods

society People living and working together in a country in an ordered way

sway Influenced

throttle Slow the flow of power

uprising A revolt

utility An organization bringing a service to a community

vital Absolutely necessary

SOURCE NOTES

QUOTATIONS

Page 5: Khurpi: http://khurpi.com/attacking-net-neutrality-is-only-happening-to-maximize-profits-of-big-telecom-companies

Page 11: Dissemble: "Is Repealing Net Neutrality Undemocratic?" https://dissemble.wordpress.com/2017/12/17/is-repealing-net-neutrality-undemocratic

Page 14: NPR: "Net Neutrality: The Long View." www.npr.org/2017/11/26/566634761/net-neutrality-the-long-view

Page 18: Newsweek: "John Oliver Explains Why Net Neutrality is in Trouble under Trump." www.newsweek.com/john-oliver-last-week-tonight-net-neutrality-596163

Page 20: Wharton: "What Will Happen if the FCC Abandons Net Neutrality?" http://knowledge.wharton.upenn.edu/article/net-neutrality-debate

Page 25: BOE magazine: "Making a Success of Online Shopping." www.boemagazine.com/2014/08/making-a-success-of-online-shopping-interview-with-shopstyle-director

Page 27: Spark: "Net Neutrality and the Path Ahead." http://spark.spit.ac.in/index.php/2017/12/29/net-neutrality-and-the-path-ahead

Page 35: Investopedia: "What is Google's Stance on Net Neutrality?" www.investopedia.com/articles/investing/060215/googles-stance-net-neutrality.asp

Page 38: RadioFreeEurope: "Explainer: Why Other Countries Care That The U.S. Ditched Net Neutrality." www.rferl.org/a/united-states-Internet-neutrality-explainer/28920398.html

REFERENCES USED FOR THIS BOOK

Chapter 1: For or Against Net Neutrality? pp. 4-7
Addiction Blog: "Why do people use the Internet?" http://Internet.addictionblog.org/why-do-people-use-the-Internet-10-reasons

Odyssey: "What's Net Neutrality & Why You Should Care About It." www.theodysseyonline.com/whats-net-neutrality-should-care-about

Vox: "The companies lobbying furiously against strong net neutrality in one chart." www.vox.com/xpress/2014/11/12/7196761/net-neutrality-lobbying

Chapter 2: How to Get Informed pp. 8-13
Reappropriate: "#AAPI groups OCA & JACL join other major civil rights orgs against net neutrality." https://bit.ly/2yoKMit

Max Wolf: "The Data From Our Comments to the FCC About Net Neutrality." http://minimaxir.com/2014/08/comments-about-comments

The Hill: "Internet's biggest players duck net neutrality fight." https://bit.ly/2qYlLDz

Chapter 3: What is Net Neutrality? pp. 14-19
ACLU: "What is net neutrality? www.aclu.org/issues/free-speech/Internet-speech/what-net-neutrality

Quarty: "Tracing the byzantine maze of the companies that have come to control America's Internet." https://bit.ly/2lEvxDf

SCRIBD: "Net Neutrality Hearing Transcript." www.scribd.com/document/24257930/Net-Neutrality-Hearing-Transcript

Chapter 4: Information Literacy pp. 20-29
The Bronx Chronicle: "To Protect Net Neutrality, Schumer, Gillibrand Call to Reclassify Broadband as a Utility." https://bit.ly/2K4whFe

Opstart: "13 Stats and Facts about Online Shopping in Canada." www.opstart.ca/13-stats-facts-online-shopping-canada

Inhabit: "Facebook's solar-powered drone took its first flight last month." https://bit.ly/2K2z4LM

Mother Jones: "Verizon Says It Wants to Kill Net Neutrality to Help Blind, Deaf, and Disabled People." https://bit.ly/2JOXsVo

Chapter 5: Where Things Stand pp. 30-39
ACLU: "Net Neutrality: Myths and Facts." www.aclu.org/other/net-neutrality-myths-and-facts

IEEE Spectrum: "Countries Around the World Tackled Net Neutrality in Different Ways." https://bit.ly/2kz722G

CBC: "Why Canada's net neutrality fight hasn't been as fierce as the one in the U.S." https://bit.ly/2BUKVuO

Chapter 6: Keeping Up To Date pp. 40-43
Google: "Create an Alert." https://support.google.com/websearch/answer/4815696?hl=en

Columbia Journalism Review: "How to build a healthy news diet." https://archives.cjr.org/news_literacy/you_are_what_you_read.php

FIND OUT MORE

Finding good source material on the Internet can sometimes be a challenge. When **analyzing** how reliable the information is, consider these points:

- Who is the author of the page? Is it an expert in the field or a person who experienced the event?

- Is the site well known and up to date? A page that has not been updated for several years probably has out-of-date information.

- Can you verify the facts with another site? Always double-check information.

- Have you checked all possible sites? Don't just look on the first page a search engine provides.

- Remember to try government sites and research papers.

- Have you recorded website addresses and names? Keep this data so you can backtrack later and verify the information you want to use.

WEBSITES

The Canadian Radio-television and Telecommunications Commission on net neutrality: **https://crtc.gc.ca/eng/Internet/diff.htm**

Dogo News explains net neutrality with pizza: **www.dogonews.com/2017/12/16/the-us-federal-communication-corporation-repeals-net-neutrality**

An animated guide to how the Internet works: **https://Internet.frontier.com/how-the-Internet-works**

BOOKS

Buzzeo, Toni. *But I Read It on the Internet!* Upstart Books, 2013.

Mapua, Jeff. *Net Neutrality and What It Means to You.* Rosen Books, 2017.

Smibert, Angie. *The Internet.* Focus Readers, 2017.

Suen, Anastasia. *Communicating in the Digital World.* Crabtree Publishing, 2018.

Swanson, Jennifer. *How the Internet Works.* Child's World, 2011.

ABOUT THE AUTHOR

Natalie Hyde has written more than 75 fiction and nonfiction books for children on all types of subjects.

INDEX